Cats

CONTENTS

cat flap

Some cats are tame.

2

lion

lioness

Some cats are wild.

panther

Some cats are big.

Siamese

Some cats are small.

4

tiger

silver tabby

Some cats have stripes.

spotted tabby

cheetah

Some cats have spots

All cats have sharp teeth.

paw

claws

scratching post

All cats have sharp claws.

lion cubs

All cats like to play.

lioness

wildebeest

All cats hunt.

leopard

domestic cat

All cats can climb.

All cats feed their babies.

All cats wash their babies.

All cats carry their babies.